DOCTOR · WHO

BBC Children's Books
Published by the Penguin Group
Penguin Books Ltd, 80 Strand, London, WC2R 0RL, England
Penguin Group (USA) Inc., 375 Hudson Street, New York, New York 10014, USA
Penguin Books (Australia) Ltd, 250 Camberwell Road, Camberwell,
Victoria 3124, Australia (A division of Pearson Australia Group Pty Ltd)
Canada, India, New Zealand, South Africa

Published by BBC Children's Books, 2007
Text and design © Children's Character Books, 2007
Pages 20-21 written by Duncan Howe
Pages 30-31 written by Matthew Kemp
Pages 10-19 and 40-46 written by Davey Moore
Pages 6-7, 24-28, 36-39 and 50-51 written by Justin Richards
Pages 10-15 and 40-46 illustrations by John Ross
Pages 10-15 and 40-46 colours by James Offredi

10 9 8 7 6 5 4 3 2 1

ISBN-13: 978-1-40590-355-4
Printed in Italy

CONTENTS

EVERYTHING CHANGES — EVEN THE DOCTOR.

Not so long ago he was a different person — really a different person. Then, after he saved Rose Tyler by absorbing the deadly energy of the Time Vortex from her, he had to regenerate. The Time Lords' way of cheating death. And it isn't just the Doctor himself who has changed, he has lost Rose. She is safe enough, living with her mum Jackie and her dad Pete, and still friends with Mickey. But she is trapped in another universe - on another world very like our own and yet so different. The biggest difference, the most important difference, is that Rose and the Doctor can never see each other again. The Doctor was forced to close all the openings between our universe and Rose's.

The openings were created by the Daleks in their Void Ship as they hid away in the space between the different universes. Gaps that the Cybermen used to come through from their world to invade ours. And gaps that were draining the life out of the universes and which would eventually destroy them — unless the Doctor closed them up. And by doing that, he was separated from Rose forever.

The Doctor managed to keep one last gap open long enough to say goodbye. He met Rose on a beach for a tearful last farewell. But even though Rose was really there, the Doctor wasn't. It was just an image of him, a picture. And pretty soon that flickered and faded, leaving Rose alone in her universe and the Doctor alone in ours. As the Doctor knows better than most life forms, nothing lasts forever.

MOVING ON...

It was time to move on, and the Doctor soon met Donna Noble — mysteriously transported into the TARDIS when she was supposed to be at church getting married. Together with Donna, the Doctor fought and defeated the terrible Empress of the Racnoss. But that was enough excitement for Donna, and she turned down the Doctor's invitation to travel with him.

NEW FRIENDS AND OLD

So the Doctor was pleased when his new friend Martha Jones accepted his offer of just one trip in the amazing TARDIS. Martha met the Doctor in the hospital where she worked, when the whole building was stolen and taken to the moon! Before long she found herself trying to escape from the Judoon and being attacked by an alien Plasmavore disguised as one of the patients.

After that, Martha probably thought a trip in the TARDIS would be a nice quiet holiday. But, of course, it wasn't. After meeting Shakespeare and being attacked by Carrionites from another dimension, the Doctor suggested just one more trip — this time to the future. Which turned out to be just as exciting and dangerous!

It's all new to Martha, but the Doctor has been battling against enemies like the gruesome Macra and the Daleks all through history. He still finds it just as exciting, whoever is with him and wherever he is.

JACK'S BACK

Martha can never meet Rose, but she has met up with another old friend of the Doctor's — Captain Jack Harkness. Waiting for years in Cardiff in the hope that the Doctor would return and refuel the TARDIS from the Time Rift there, Captain Jack was desperate to find the Doctor again. He even clung to the side of the TARDIS as it travelled through time and space. Rose had used the power of the Time Vortex to bring Jack back to life after he was exterminated by the Daleks — and now he can't be killed. When the Doctor met another figure from his past, the Master, the fact that Jack was indestructible turned out to be a big help!

And the Doctor discovered the old meaning of the message he was given by the Face of Boe before it died. It was said the Face would tell a great secret to a wandering traveller, and sure enough it had a final message for the Doctor — a message he couldn't bring himself to believe: 'You Are Not Alone.' Now the Doctor knows what that meant...

WAY BACK AT THE DAWN OF THE UNIVERSE, THE ETERNALS FOUND THE RIGHT WORD TO BANISH THE CARRIONITES INTO THE DEEP DARKNESS. NOBODY WAS EVER SURE IF THEY WERE REAL OR A MYTH, UNTIL SHAKESPEARE'S WORDS ALLOWED THEM TO ESCAPE AND ATTEMPT TO CREATE A NEW WORLD OF BLOOD AND WITCHCRAFT ON EARTH.

Claws for attacking their human victims.

Rows of sharp shark-like teeth.

MotherDoomfinger can kill with a single touch.

Can fly with or without a broomstick.

Mother Bloodtide and Mother Doomfinger are only ever seen in their true form.

Use psychic energy to communicate when they're apart.

Lilith is a beautiful young girl in her human guise, but she is really a hideous hag.

DALEK WORDSEARCH

TIME AFTER TIME THE DOCTOR HAS BATTLED AGAINST THE DALEKS. HELP HIM RID THIS GRID OF DALEKS BY FINDING ALL THE DALEK-RELATED WORDS. THEY MAY BE HIDDEN HORIZONTALLY, VERTICALLY OR DIAGONALLY.

W	R	Y	I	O	P	L	G	D	A	C	N	M	V	E
X	I	C	U	L	T	O	H	J	K	R	T	S	T	B
M	F	A	Z	G	Y	U	T	F	R	D	E	A	E	N
R	S	A	O	O	D	A	L	U	J	H	N	C	R	V
G	E	N	E	S	I	S	A	R	K	I	P	O	P	I
K	C	D	M	F	N	O	P	E	M	G	E	D	S	L
J	A	S	P	T	H	A	L	R	S	C	A	J	A	N
S	K	Z	E	K	L	A	E	B	K	J	S	A	T	S
E	C	F	R	Y	D	T	B	V	A	J	L	S	Y	O
T	G	R	O	A	X	Y	S	K	R	I	E	T	S	M
A	H	K	R	E	N	E	W	Y	O	R	K	E	M	E
S	A	A	D	U	Y	T	R	E	S	D	G	H	N	B
K	L	D	Y	P	I	G	S	L	A	V	E	S	S	

CAAN, CULT, DALEK, EMPEROR, EXTERMINATE, GENESIS ARK, JAST, NEW YORK, PIG SLAVES, SEC, SKARO, THAL, THAY.

"FOR A LONG TIME NOW, MOUNTAIN GOATHERDS HAVE BEEN LOSING THEIR GOATS. NOT LOSING THEM TO WOLVES AND FINDING THEIR RAGGED REMAINS, BUT TURNING AWAY FROM THEM FOR A MOMENT - ONLY TO FIND A FULL GROWN GOAT HAS GONE, AS THOUGH SNATCHED FROM THE AIR."

THERE WAS TALK OF THIEVES AND BANDITS, HIDING IN THE CAVES UP ON THE MOUNTAIN. BUT SUCH A GROUP WOULD SURELY HAVE COME DOWN TO THE STREAMS TO DRINK AND BATHE AND NO ONE HAS EVER ADMITTED TO SEEING SUCH A THING.

WE'RE NOT GOING TO MAKE KINDLING BY NIGHTFALL. WE'D BETTER SET UP CAMP. SEE IF YOU CAN FIND SOME FIREWOOD. I'LL TELL YOU THE REST LATER.

COOL! THIS'LL BE LIKE THE SUMMER CAMP I NEVER HAD!

SO WHAT DO YOU RECKON? I'VE SEEN SOME STUFF ON MY TRAVELS WITH YOU. BUT DRAGONS? THEY'RE JUST A MYTH, RIGHT? JUST A STORY.

THERE'S ALWAYS A REASON FOR A STORY TO EXIST. YOU KNOW - NO SMOKE WITHOUT FIRE.

...OR FIREWOOD! COME ON, GET GATHERING!

ARE YOU SURE WE'RE GOING TO BE ALRIGHT OUT HERE TONIGHT?

AS LONG AS WE STICK TO THE WET LOWLANDS. THIS I WHY I TAKE THE LONG PATH THROUGH THE MARSHES. TRADESMEN LIKE MYSEL RISKS LOSING HI SUPPLIES - EVEN HIS HORS - IN THE MUD AND THE MIST BUT AT LEAST I STAND CHANCE OF SURVIVIN THE JOURNEY

"NOT LIKE THE TRAVELLERS AND TRADESMEN WHO LEFT THEIR HOMES AND MADE THEIR WAY BETWEEN THE TWO TOWNS ON THE MOUNTAIN PATH, NEVER TO REACH THEIR DESTINATION."

"THEIR BELONGINGS WOULD SOMETIMES BE FOUND, BUT THERE WOULD BE NO SIGN OF THE MAN HIMSELF. SURELY THIS COULD NOT BE THE WORK OF OTHER MEN?"

A SURVIVOR'S HANDBOOK

Should you ever find yourself a passenger on-board the TARDIS, you might want to memorise these instructions on how to cope with some of the worst the universe can throw at you...

HOW TO ESCAPE FROM A RAXACORICOFALLAPATORIAN

To defeat a Raxacoricofallapatorian, it helps to know a few basic facts:

- Raxacoricofallapatorians are creatures of living calcium.

- They have a highly developed sense of smell.

- Members of the same family are psychically linked and can sense if harm comes to one of their own.

- Female Raxacoricofallapatorians have a poisoned claw that can be fired like a dart, and they can fell you with an exhalation of poisoned breath.

So, how to escape when Raxacoricofallapatorians attack? Vinegar goes well with chips, but not so well with Raxacoricofallapatorians. Acetic acid is the organic chemical compound that gives vinegar its distinctive taste — but it will melt a Raxacoricofallapatorian. If there's no vinegar to hand, you could always try other acidic foodstuffs such as cola or tomato sauce. The effect may be less dramatic but the ensuing food fight might just buy you enough time to escape. If you successfully defeat a Raxacoricofallapatorian, then don't hang around enjoying your moment of triumph. Other members of its family will probably be on their way to get you! If all else fails — leg it. Considering their bulk, Raxacoricofallapatorians are pretty fast runners — but they're not exactly svelte. Even with their compression field activated, they'll have trouble following you under a low hedge or through a small window.

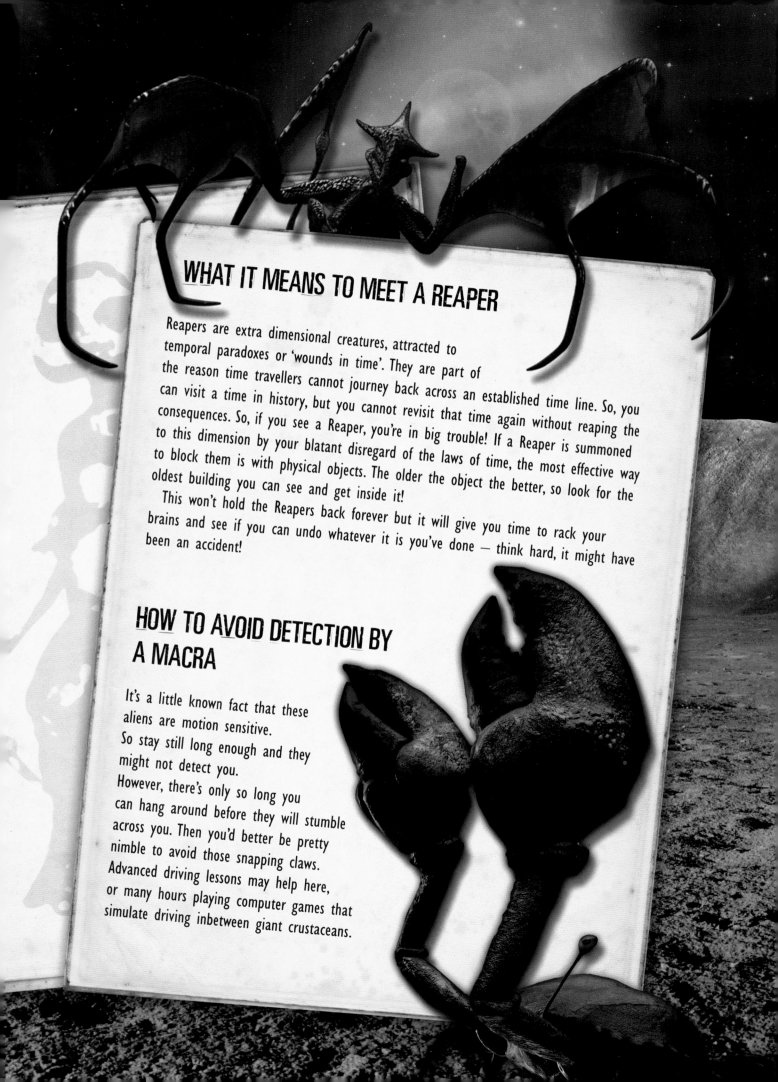

WHAT IT MEANS TO MEET A REAPER

Reapers are extra dimensional creatures, attracted to temporal paradoxes or 'wounds in time'. They are part of the reason time travellers cannot journey back across an established time line. So, you can visit a time in history, but you cannot revisit that time again without reaping the consequences. So, if you see a Reaper, you're in big trouble! If a Reaper is summoned to this dimension by your blatant disregard of the laws of time, the most effective way to block them is with physical objects. The older the object the better, so look for the oldest building you can see and get inside it!

This won't hold the Reapers back forever but it will give you time to rack your brains and see if you can undo whatever it is you've done — think hard, it might have been an accident!

HOW TO AVOID DETECTION BY A MACRA

It's a little known fact that these aliens are motion sensitive.

So stay still long enough and they might not detect you.

However, there's only so long you can hang around before they will stumble across you. Then you'd better be pretty nimble to avoid those snapping claws. Advanced driving lessons may help here, or many hours playing computer games that simulate driving inbetween giant crustaceans.

WHAT TO DO IF YOU SEE A KRILLITANE

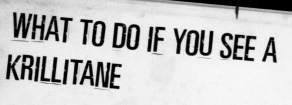

Tricky one this. Krillitanes are known as a 'composite species'. This means that they take the best physical parts of any species they conquer and adapt them to suit themselves. Creepy, isn't it? And that's just what Krillitanes are — creepy! They could look different every time you see them. In fact, you could be sitting next to one right now...

The best way to thwart an attacking Krillitane is with Krillitane oil. A small amount can boost your intelligence, but a whole barrel of it is unstable and corrosive. If you're in possession of a laser, shoot the barrel and you'll defeat the Krillitane.

If you haven't got a laser, you'd better just run.

HOW TO GET RID OF A RACNOSS

One way to rid a planet of a Racnoss is to sluice it down the nearest drain with hundreds of thousands of gallons of water. This, however, might not always be possible. In which case, there is another way:

- Find a giant jam jar.

- Place the giant jam jar over the Racnoss, making sure not to trap any of its legs.

- Lift up the rim of the jam jar ever so slightly. Slide a massive postcard underneath the Racnoss, being careful not to shudder when then Racnoss runs up the side of the jam jar.

- With both hands, pick up the whole lot and hop from one foot to another, while saying "Racnoss! Racnoss!" and nodding towards the nearest enormous window, indicating that someone should open it for you.

If no one is present to open a window, then you'd better hope that you haven't locked the front door as you use your elbow to push down the handle.

HOW TO ESCAPE FROM A BLACK HOLE

Nothing can escape from a black hole. Not even light. Which means you can't even see them without having your eyeballs sucked out. Probably.

However, Time Lords practically invented black holes. So the only sensible advice that can be given to you here is make sure you're with a Time Lord if you're going to go around looking into black holes.

HOW TO COOK A KRYNOID

The most important thing to remember when cooking with Krynoids, is to make sure you eat it, before it eats you. Although its home planet remains unknown, Krynoid seeds arrive here from space and can remain dormant for thousands of years before being activated by ultraviolet light. Once it has germinated, a Krynoid plant will attempt to mingle its DNA with other life forms and transform them into Krynoids. As terrifying as a fully-grown Krynoid plant can be, it does make perfect light and fluffy fritters — which are just delicious when served with a side of sweet chilli dipping sauce. Get an adult to give you a hand with the cooking and have a go at home:

- Separate the Krynoid leaves from the stalk. Parboil the leaves and discard the tough stalk.

- For every cup of Krynoid leaves, add half a cup of flour, a teaspoon of baking powder, one cup of milk and season to taste.

- Mix until ingredients are just combined.

- Drop palm-sized patties of the mixture into hot oil and cook 1 to 2 minutes on each side.

- Drain on paper towels.

The whole process must be undertaken quickly as Krynoid plants can exert telepathic control over other plant life in the surrounding area, and if you're not quick enough you may find your peace lily looming over your shoulder brandishing an egg whisk.

LOOK UP INTO THE NIGHT SKY AND WHAT DO YOU SEE? IT'S MOSTLY STARS, AND IF YOU HAVE GOOD EYES, YOU MIGHT BE ABLE TO SEE ABOUT 4,000 OF THEM. BUT IN OUR GALAXY, THE MILKY WAY, THERE ARE AT LEAST 200,000,000,000 STARS IN ALL!

The closest star to Earth is our sun, a type of star that's very common in our galaxy, but the Doctor has seen some very strange stars on his travels through the universe...

THE SUN

Surface Temperature: 5,800 degrees
Diameter: 1,390,000km
Distance from Earth: 149,600,00 km

Deep in the core of Earth's nearest star, about 700,000,000 tonnes of hydrogen are converted into helium every second. The energy released by this heats up the whole Sun. The dark sunspots you can sometimes see are actually areas that are 2,000 degrees cooler than their surroundings. Although the sunspots look small, our Earth could fit inside one! Our Sun is about 4.5 billion years old, and is only middle-aged. In about 5 billion years it will run out of hydrogen fuel, and you really don't want to be around when that happens!

BETELGEUSE

Surface Temperature: 3,600 degrees
Diameter: 521,962,500km
Distance from Earth: 427 light years

Betelgeuse is a red giant star. This star is enormous, about 300 million of our suns could fit inside it. In about 5 billion years time, the Earth's Sun will turn into a red giant. It will swell up, not as big as Betelgeuse, but big enough to swallow the Earth! The Ninth Doctor and Rose travelled forwards in time and watched this happen from Platform One.

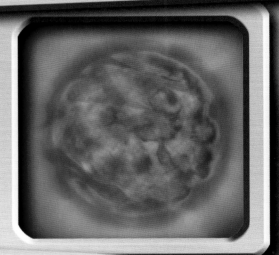

Surface Temperature: 25,000 degrees
Diameter: 11,700km
Distance from Earth: 8.6 light years

SIRIUS B

Sirius B is the smallest of a pair of stars and is what astronomers call a white dwarf. White dwarfs are only about the size of Earth, but they often still weigh about the same as our sun. This means one spoonful of white dwarf material could weigh about as much as an elephant! Our Sun will go from being a red giant into a white dwarf, the last change it will make. After this, over billions of years, it will just cool down and gradually fade from view.

Surface temperature: 520,000 degrees
Diameter: 20km
Distance from Earth: 552 light years

GEMINGA

This very strange star was once much bigger than our sun, but is now very tiny - only about 20km across! A very large star at the end of its life doesn't form a white dwarf, it collapses, triggering a huge explosion. An explosion so big it can shine brighter than the whole galaxy. What remains behind after the dust has settled is a neutron star. A teaspoon of neutron star could weigh a billion tonnes. That's more than the weight of everyone on the planet!

Surface Temperature: Zero, nothing can get out, not even heat
Diameter of event horizon: 60km
Distance from Earth: 10,000 light years

CYGNUS X-1

Cygnus X-1 was once a very big star, maybe ten times heavier than our Sun. When it ran out of hydrogen fuel and collapsed, it didn't form a white dwarf or a neutron star, it formed a black hole. Black holes are some of the strangest and scariest objects in the universe. They weigh so much that their gravity is so strong nothing can escape. Not even light, which means you can't see them! Astronomers only found Cygnus X-1 because it has a companion star which it is slowly eating. If you get too close to a black hole by accident and cross what's called the event horizon, you'll disappear inside and get crushed down to nothing! It's thought there is a gigantic black hole in the centre of the Milky Way, millions of times heavier than our sun and so big it can gobble up whole stars!

The stars are so far away, it is tricky to write the distance down. What astronomers usually do is measure distance in what we call light years. Light is the fastest thing in the universe, and in one year it can travel 9,460,730,472,580 km, a distance hard to imagine! One of the fastest man-made objects, the Voyager 1 space probe, is moving at 63,000km an hour. At this speed it would take 73,000 years to reach the nearest star, Proxima Centauri, which is 4.2 light years away. Of course the TARDIS can travel light years in no time at all!

ONCE KNOWN AS THE LONELY ASSASSINS, THE WEEPING ANGELS HAVE THE MOST PERFECT DEFENCE SYSTEM EVER EVOLVED: THEY'RE QUANTUM LOCKED, WHICH MEANS THEY DON'T EXIST WHEN THEY CAN BE SEEN. AS SOON AS THEY ARE SEEN BY ANY OTHER CREATURE, THEY FREEZE INTO ROCK.

Usually seen with their hands over their faces, not weeping, but just not looking at each other.

The touch of an Angel zaps you back into the past and lets you live to death. You die in the past, and in the present they consume the energy of the days you might have had.

The energy from the TARDIS would have allowed the Angels to feast forever.

A Weeping Angel can only attack when it can't be seen - so if you come across one, don't blink!

The Weeping Angels waited for Sally in Wester Drumlins House.

WATCH HUNT

HELP MARTHA RETURN THE DOCTOR TO HIS TIME LORD SELF. ONE PATH WILL TAKE HER TO HIS WATCH, BUT THE OTHERS WILL LEAD HER STRAIGHT INTO THE HANDS OF THE FAMILY OF BLOOD AND THE SCARECROWS!

THE PLANET THAT WEPT

The dew dripped from the trees by the beach like teardrops. Twin suns sparkled on the azure waters. Martha Jones stretched out on her towel, wriggling to flatten the silky sand underneath. A shadow fell across her face and she opened her eyes.

'Strange planet this,' the Doctor said. He was kicking gently at the sand close by. 'No life.' He sniffed. 'Well, no intelligent life.' He raised his eyebrows. 'Well, no intelligent life to speak of.'

'I take it you're not including us?' Martha said.

'Super-intelligent, us. Off the scale. You know, it's half water and half land. Jungle mainly. Rainforest. Difficult to know if the land is an island in a great big blue sea, or the water is a lake in a great big green continent.'

'Don't care,' Martha told him. 'So long as I can get some rays.'

'You won't get a tan,' the Doctor said. 'No ultraviolet. Safe, though.'

'I just like the warmth,' she told him. 'And the light. Lying on a deserted beach with the waves lapping the shore and a tropical jungle behind us. That's what travel should be about.'

The Doctor sniffed and looked round. He was still wearing his suit, hands thrust deep into the pockets. 'That's not travel,' he said. 'You need movement for travel. A bit of energy. A bit of excitement. Deserted beach on a deserted planet. Not much excitement here. And we all need a bit of excitement.'

'A bit of being chased by monsters and attacked by maniacs,' Martha said.

'I thought you enjoyed it.' He sounded hurt.

Martha sighed and sat up. 'I do. But now and again it's nice to have a break. Chill out.'

'In the hot sun.'

She laughed. 'If you'd stop blocking it out, yeah.'

'Sorry.' He didn't move.

'Why don't you go for a walk or something? Or better still, serve drinks?'

'Good idea.' He drew circles in the soft sand with the toe of his shoe. 'Think I'll have a wander through the cool shade of the forest.'

'Jungle,' Martha corrected him.

'Whatever.' He was already striding purposefully towards the edge of the jungle. Soon the beach was empty, except for Martha, her towel, and the reassuring dark blue shape of the TARDIS.

Martha stretched out again and soaked up the warmth of the suns. They were more orange than yellow, less dazzling than Earth's sun. Which was nice. Well, it was all nice. Martha drifted into a peaceful sleep.

'Martha...'

She stirred in her sleep. Murmured. Drifted off again.

Slightly louder now: 'Martha....'

And Martha's eyes flickered open. She yawned, stretched and sat up.

'Martha.'

The voice was faint. Barely more than a whisper. Like the wind in the nearby trees. Martha looked round. But there was no one in sight. 'Doctor? Is that you?' She stood up and dusted sand from her arms. She must have imagined it. The breeze in the jungle, moving the leaves.

'Martha.'

Martha froze. It was definitely a voice, and definitely calling for her.

'Doctor?' she called again. It hadn't sounded like him. But he'd said the planet was deserted. No intelligent life at all. 'Is that you?' she called again, but slightly hesitant now. Slightly nervous. 'Stop mucking about.' She walked slowly towards the edge of the jungle. The sand gave way gradually to palm trees and long-bladed grass.

And the voice came from somewhere in amongst the trees. 'Martha...'

'It's all a bit green for me,' the Doctor announced to the jungle. He squelched his way across a narrow stream, and paused for breath at the top of a hill.

The jungle was quite dense once you got into it. Trees and shrubs pressing in on all sides. A canopy of green filtered the suns' light so that the ground was dappled and it was difficult to make out details in the gloom.

The Doctor had to get quite close to a tree before he could see the detail of the trunk. He didn't recognise the type, but the bark was interesting. Lines and whirls and textures. He traced his finger on the trunk, following the ridges and troughs.

'Funny how you can make out patterns that aren't really there,' he murmured. 'I mean, this could almost be a face.'

He gave a laugh, tapped at where the eyes might be, traced the mouth. Ran his finger down the side of the nose. Yes, if you used a bit of imagination, it could be a face.

Then the face in the bark of the tree opened its eyes.

The Doctor took a step backwards, and almost lost his footing.

'I knew you'd come, Doctor,' the face in the tree said.

The voice seemed to be just ahead of her all the time. Martha made her way cautiously through the jungle.

'Who are you?' she called. 'What do you want? If that's you, Doctor, then I can tell you this isn't funny. Just because you're bored...'

Martha looked back. She could just see the edge of the jungle, where the light was slightly brighter. A little way further, but no more. She didn't fancy getting lost in an alien jungle.

'Martha...'

She passed a line of trees, long thin leaves hanging down like a curtain. Martha had to push them aside to get through. And there in front of her was a pool of water. More than a pool, a small lake. The water was as clear and blue as the sea.

'Look, whoever you are,' Martha called out. 'That's enough, all right? I'm going back to the beach now.'

She looked round, half expecting someone to step out from the trees and stand beside the pool with her. More than half expecting it to be the Doctor. But there was no one.

Martha sighed, and stooped down by the pool, staring into clear water. She could see the vague shape of her reflection staring back at her. She waved at it.

The reflection did not wave back.

And now that Martha looked more closely, she saw it was a woman, pale and beautiful. It was not Martha's face rippling on the water's surface at all. She spun round, but there was no one there. No one at all. Just Martha, and the face in the water.

'Don't go, Martha,' the face said.

She turned and ran.

There were faces everywhere now. Eyes stared up at Martha from the ground. The bark of the trees was watching her. She pushed aside a long leaf that stared back at her.

She tried to look straight ahead as she ran back towards the beach. Tried not to look at the faces.

Which was why she didn't see the figure beside her, until he took her hand.

'Run!' the Doctor told her. 'Back to the TARDIS, now.'

'Those faces,' Martha gasped. 'Can you see them?'

'Yes.'

'Do you know what they are?'

'Yes.'

'And?'

'And we need to keep running.'

They burst out of the jungle and on to the beach. Out of breath, Martha was slowing, gasping for breath. It was harder running on the sand, her feet sinking in. The TARDIS was a dark blot on the silver beach far away.

'There was a face in a tree,' the Doctor said. They had slowed to a fast walk. He was still holding her hand. 'It told me what happened here.' He turned to look at Martha as they hurried on, and she thought he looked sad.

She was getting her breath back now. 'You said there was no life here, no one at all.'

'But there was once. A great civilisation. Well, maybe great isn't the right word. They didn't take care of their home, this planet. War, pollution, toxic waste... The environment began to collapse and they never even noticed, not until it was too late.'

Martha looked round at the beautiful beach, the lush vegetation... 'What happened?'

'Things got out of control. Reached a tipping point. One day it started to rain.' The Doctor stopped and turned to face Martha. 'Acid rain. It rained for a hundred years, and the people and their civilisation — buildings, cars, everything — dissolved. Washed away for ever.'

Martha just stared at him. 'That's...' She shook her head, unable to think of a word big enough to describe the tragedy. 'But what about the faces? The voices calling us?'

The Doctor looked up at the sky. The faintest wisp of a cloud was drifting high above them. 'Somehow the people became part of the rain. They were washed into the soil and the lakes and taken up in the roots of the trees.'

Another cloud drifted in front of one of the suns, and the Doctor quickened his pace. 'We need to hurry,' he said. 'The people are part of the planet now, a collective mind, for millions of years, evolving and coexisting with nature.'

'Friends of the Earth,' Martha muttered. 'So, why the rush?'

'Millions of years,' the Doctor said. 'Think of that. Have you any idea what that means? I mean, you might have enjoyed lazing about on the beach just now, but would you want to do it for a million years or more?'

'I think the novelty would wear off.' The TARDIS still seemed a long way off. The light was dimming as the sky clouded over.

'And the novelty has worn off,' the Doctor said. 'Worn off and been forgotten. That's what the face in the tree told me. It's all just so boring. The whole population of the planet has run out of things to say. Nothing left to talk about. No more stories to tell.' He shook his head as if the enormity of this had only just struck him. 'A world where they've run out of stories, how sad is that?' He took her hand again and started to run.

Martha nodded. 'So why are we running?'

'Because they want us to join them. They want us to tell them new stories. The water in the seas, the sand on the beach, it all heard us talking. It knows we can tell them new stories that will ease the boredom.'

The sky flickered as lightning flashed across it. Not far now — the TARDIS was maybe twenty metres away...

'That isn't so bad. You're great at stories.'

'Maybe. But do you want to become a mountain stream, or a leaf on a tree or a grain of sand on the beach, or a whisper in the wind?'

'You're kidding, right?' But she gripped his hand more tightly and ran faster.

'We have to get to the TARDIS, before it starts to — '

The boom of thunder drowned his words. The first drops of rain splashed down on the beach. The sand fizzed and melted where the acid fell.

Ten metres away.

'Don't let it touch you!' the Doctor yelled above the breaking storm. He had the TARDIS key out ready — aiming for the lock as they raced the last few metres. A drop of rain hit the Doctor's sleeve and his coat steamed and spat as the acid ate into it.

Then the door was open, and the Doctor was pushing Martha into the TARDIS. A moment later, he was inside too, as the storm finally broke and the rain lashed down on the empty beach.

The Doctor stood in the open door of the TARDIS, looking out at the storm. He watched the rain falling, the clouds swirling, the trees swaying in the wind. Then he reached out his hand, and let a single drop of rain splash into his palm.

His face contorted with the pain, as the water boiled and the skin blistered. The Doctor turned his hand and shook the raindrop free, letting it fall onto the sand outside.

The TARDIS slowly faded away, the sound of its engines lost in the howl of the storm. Millions of drops of rain were falling from the sky like teardrops. Inside each raindrop was a tiny image of the Doctor, smiling sadly as he started his first story. And as it listened, the planet continued to weep.

THE END

THE FAMILY CHASED THE DOCTOR THROUGH TIME AND SPACE USING A TIME AGENT'S VORTEX MANIPULATOR. THEIR LIFE FORCE WAS RUNNING OUT AND THEY WANTED THE ENERGY OF THE TARDIS TO ENABLE THEM TO LIVE FOREVER. THE DOCTOR MADE SURE THEY GOT THEIR WISH, BUT NOT IN QUITE THE WAY THEY WANTED...

Brother was suspended in time inside a scarecrow.

He imprisoned the Mother in an event horizon.

The Family need human bodies to give them shape.

Sister was trapped in mirrors.

The Doctor wrapped the Father in unbreakable chains.

The Family used molecular fringe animation to create an army of scarecrows.

THE LAST GREAT TIME WAR SAW THE TOTAL DESTRUCTION OF THE TIME LORDS – WITH ONE KNOWN EXCEPTION: THE DOCTOR. HE HAS TRAVELLED THROUGH TIME KNOWING THAT HE IS ALONE IN THE UNIVERSE...UNTIL NOW.

'You are not alone' — the mysterious last words from the Face of Boe gave hope to the lonely traveller, haunted by the knowledge that everyone he knew died in the battle against the Daleks. But the Doctor's childhood friend the Master also survived the Time War — news which didn't please the kind-hearted Time Lord as much as you'd expect! For while the Doctor uses his powers for good, the Master has left a trail of destruction behind him. The two were friends at school, so the Master knows the Doctor's strengths and weaknesses better than anyone. But what makes the Master so dangerous?

MASTER OF... EVIL

As you'd expect from a man who can summon the Devil himself, the Master is...well, a master in black magic and the dark arts. He is happy to work with other powerful beings in his attempts to control the universe. In the past, he has teamed up with the Nestene Consciousness and the Daleks to try and take over the Earth, with only the Doctor's quick thinking saving the human race from extinction.

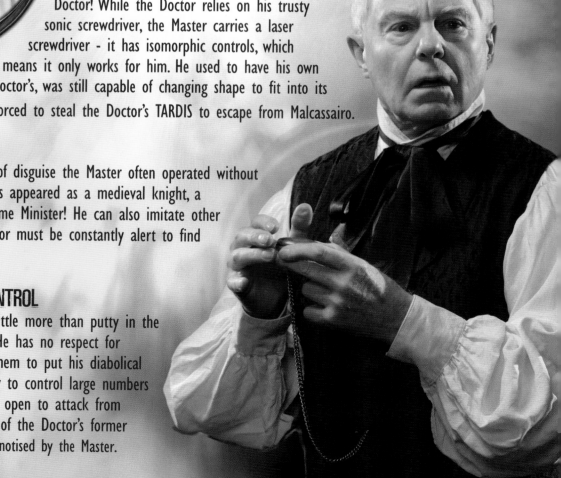

MASTER OF... TECHNOLOGY

The Master's most powerful weapon is his intelligence. Believe it or not, he actually has a higher degree in cosmic science than the Doctor! While the Doctor relies on his trusty sonic screwdriver, the Master carries a laser screwdriver - it has isomorphic controls, which means it only works for him. He used to have his own TARDIS, which, unlike the Doctor's, was still capable of changing shape to fit into its surroundings. But he was forced to steal the Doctor's TARDIS to escape from Malcassairo.

MASTER OF... DISGUISE

Using his amazing powers of disguise the Master often operated without the Doctor's knowledge. He's appeared as a medieval knight, a Reverend, and even the Prime Minister! He can also imitate other people's voices, so the Doctor must be constantly alert to find his old enemy.

MASTER OF... MIND CONTROL

The weak human mind is little more than putty in the Master's controlling hands. He has no respect for Earthlings and often uses them to put his diabolical plans into action. His ability to control large numbers of people leaves the Doctor open to attack from anyone, with at least three of the Doctor's former companions having been hypnotised by the Master.

MASTER OF... REGENERATION

All Time Lords have a maximum of twelve regenerations — but not the Master. After carelessly using up all of his regenerations, he transported himself into the body of a Trakenite and began the cycle once more. Even death cannot stop him. After the Master was executed by the Daleks, the Eighth Doctor agreed to carry his ashes back to the Time Lords' home planet of Gallifrey. The ashes transformed into a blob, which escaped the TARDIS and took over an ambulance driver! The Doctor thought he had finally destroyed his former classmate when the Master was sucked into the Eye of Harmony (a black hole which provided energy for Gallifrey, as well as powering the TARDIS), after attempting to steal the Doctor's remaining regenerations.

MASTER OF... SURPRISE

Although he may have tried to rob the Doctor of his remaining lives, the Master is also capable of surprising acts of kindness towards his old friend. The Master surprised the Doctor for the final time when he chose to die, rather than regenerate, during their latest encounter.

THE MASTER VS. THE DOCTOR A BATTLE ACROSS TIME

In the past, the Master's lust for power at all costs has always led to his downfall. He over-complicates simple plans and this short-sighted arrogance leaves his schemes in tatters. The Doctor may once have called him 'an unimaginative plodder,' but there's no doubt he holds a great respect for one of his most dangerous enemies. The feeling is mutual, with the Master recognising the talents of the only person who can stand in his way — he knows that a universe without the Doctor scarcely bears thinking about...

The two Time Lords are evenly matched, and only by confronting his greatest fears is the Doctor able to defeat the Master whenever they meet. Once again, the Doctor finds himself the last of the Time Lords...

CHRISTMAS WOULDN'T BE THE SAME WITHOUT THE DOCTOR SAVING THE PLANET FROM DESTRUCTION! BUT HOW MUCH DO YOU REMEMBER FROM HIS FESTIVE VISITS TO EARTH?

1. True or false - the Daleks have attacked London at Christmas?

2. Last Christmas, Donna mysteriously appeared in the TARDIS. What was she wearing?
A. A cowboy hat.
B. A wedding dress.
C. A reindeer costume.

3. The previous Christmas, a spaceship appeared over London. What did it look like?
A. A banana.
B. The TARDIS.
C. A big rock.

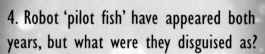

4. Robot 'pilot fish' have appeared both years, but what were they disguised as?
A. Santas with instruments.
B. Elves with pogo sticks.
C. Christmas trees.

5. Where had the Racnoss children been hiding?
A. In Christmas presents.
B. Under the sea.
C. In the centre of the Earth.

6. Which festive food did the Doctor use to defeat the Sycorax?
A. A turkey.
B. A satsuma.
C. Cranberry sauce.

7. True or false - the Empress of the Racnoss had a lair beneath Canary Wharf?

8 True or false - the Doctor made it snow for Donna?

9. What was the leader of the Racnoss called?
A. The Queen.
B. The Grand High Priestess.
C. The Empress.

10. How did the Sycorax control a third of the human race?
A. Blood control.
B. Remote control.
C. Hypnosis.

11. True or false - Donna became the Doctor's new companion after her Christmas adventure?

12. What was the name of the Racnoss' spaceship?
A. The Webship.
B. The Space Web.
C. The Webstar.

B.

A.

C.

13. Finally, look carefully through the TARDIS scanner at these scrambled images of some Christmas invaders. Do you know which is which?

Answers on page 61

CAPTAIN JACK'S CONUNDRUM

USE THE SHIFT CODE BELOW TO WORK OUT WHAT HAPPENED TO CAPTAIN JACK AFTER THE DOCTOR LEFT HIM BEHIND ON THE GAME STATION.

A shift code is one where each letter of the alphabet has moved on and been replaced by another letter. To crack the code, find the code letters in the bottom row, then replace them with the letters in the top row. For example, Captain Jack in this code would be written: LJYCJRW   SJLT

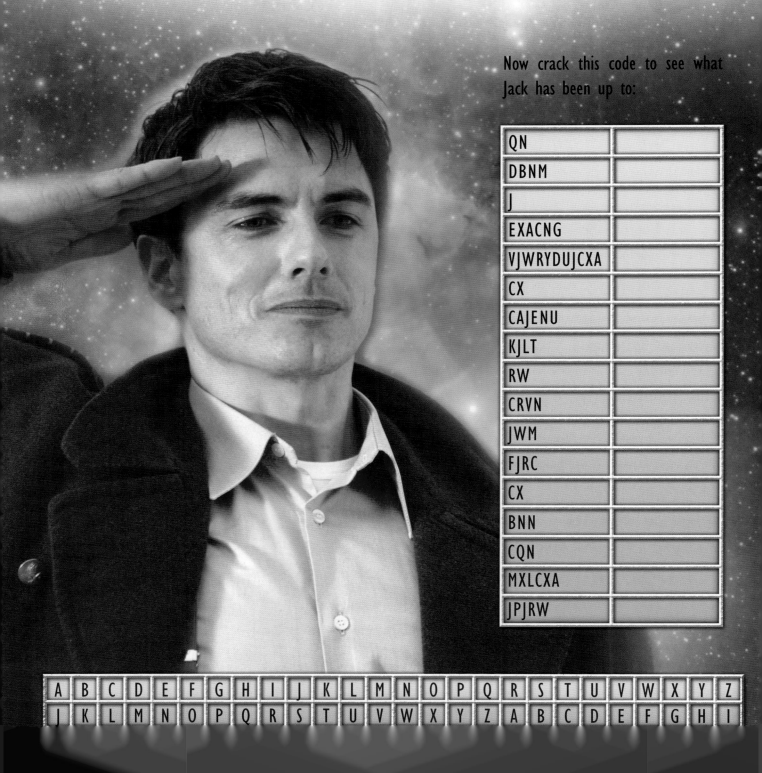

Now crack this code to see what Jack has been up to:

QN	
DBNM	
J	
EXACNG	
VJWRYDUJCXA	
CX	
CAJENU	
KJLT	
RW	
CRVN	
JWM	
FJRC	
CX	
BNN	
CQN	
MXLCXA	
JPJRW	

A	B	C	D	E	F	G	H	I	J	K	L	M	N	O	P	Q	R	S	T	U	V	W	X	Y	Z
J	K	L	M	N	O	P	Q	R	S	T	U	V	W	X	Y	Z	A	B	C	D	E	F	G	H	I

THE JUDOON ARE AN INTERPLANETARY POLICE FORCE FOR HIRE, WHO WERE LOOKING FOR THE MURDERER OF THE CHILD PRINCESS OF PADRIVOLE REGENCY NINE. WHEN THEIR SEARCH BROUGHT THEM TO EARTH, THEY USED AN H_2O SCOOP TO TAKE THE HOSPITAL WHERE THE SUSPECT WAS HIDDEN TO THE NEUTRAL TERRITORY OF THE MOON!

Helmet conceals a large, horned head.

Leathery skin.

Can assimilate languages using a device which plugs into a nozzle on their chests.

Studded leather uniforms with panelled skirts like Roman centurions.

Cataloguing scanner device for determining alien species.

The Plasmavore hid herself in the hospital by drinking people's blood in order to appear human on the Judoon scanners.

IN THE BEGINNING...

Long ago on a planet called Skaro two sides went to war. The Kaleds
other for a thousand years, but neither side was able to win. The war
sides were running out of weapons and soldiers. Finally, just two hug
protected by a massive dome. In the final days of this terrible war, th

The Kaleds put their hope of victory in a brilliant scientist called Davr
in a special bunker away from the main Kaled city. Davros had been
relied on a special chariot with built-in life support systems. But his e
even worse fate lay in store for his people.

Davros discovered that the chemical and biological weapons used in the
affected the people of both sides – slowly changing them into hideous, r
research from looking into ways of winning the war to the survival of h
machine and life support system for the creature he now
knew his people would become. He based it partly on his
own chariot, and he gave it a name — the Dalek.

THE ULTIMATE WAR MACHINE

But Davros didn't wait for the mutation to take
place. He created his own Kaled mutants, and
then he altered them — making them,
he thought, stronger and better able to
survive. He removed all emotion, all pity,
and left his creatures with only hate and an
instinct for survival. Having created the ultimate
war machine — the Dalek — he sent it to destroy
the Thals.

Davros had already arranged for the destruction of
his own people, the Kaleds, when they tried to stop
his Dalek project. Now only Davros and his scientists
remained. But he had taught the Daleks that they
were better than all other life forms, and they
decided that included Davros himself. Together
with the last scientists, he was exterminated by
his own creations.

THE DOCTOR'S GREATEST ENEMY

For many years, the Doctor fought against the Daleks and they became his greatest enemy. He helped the Thals — who had evolved and mutated into perfect humans — defeat them in their city on Skaro. He then defeated the Dalek invasion of Earth in the 22nd century and their attack on the galaxy in AD 4,000. The Daleks were so afraid of the Doctor that they sent their own time machine to pursue him through time and space.

The Doctor even managed to start a civil war on Skaro when he infected a group of Daleks with the 'human factor' so they questioned their Emperor and were attacked by the Emperor's guards... He foiled a Dalek attempt to change history and invade Earth again, and destroyed an army of invisible Daleks on the planet Spiridon. He even faced — and several times defeated — a revived Davros...

A SPECIAL MISSION

The Time Lords of Gallifrey sent the Fourth Doctor on a special mission. They sent him to Skaro to stop Davros creating the creatures they knew would one day become the dominant life form in the universe. The Doctor failed, but when the Daleks discovered that the Time Lords had tried to prevent them ever being created, the seeds of the Great Time War were sown...

THE GREAT TIME WAR

As negotiations broke down, a full-scale war erupted within the Time Vortex and beyond that in the Ultimate Void. The Time Lords reached back into history for ever more terrible weapons, while the Daleks unleashed the Deathsmiths of Goth. The War raged for centuries, unseen by most of the Universe. But the Higher Species watched and wept...

No one knows what really happened at the end of the Time War, but when it was over, a single survivor walked alone through the carnage of Gallifrey and Skaro — the Time Lord who had brought the War to its terrible end: The Doctor.

SURVIVORS

But the ripples caused by the Time War continued to spread. The Doctor was horrified to discover that not all the Daleks had been destroyed. He discovered a single surviving Dalek that had fallen through time to arrive on Earth. It was kept chained up by American billionaire Henry van Statten, but it recognised its old enemy the Doctor and was determined to escape.

The Doctor's companion Rose accidentally gave it the power it needed — the touch of a time traveller was enough to re-energize the Dalek. It broke free and exterminated hundreds of people. But as well as power, it had absorbed something else from Rose — a part of her humanity. It began to doubt itself, to question the Dalek way. The last Dalek in the universe destroyed itself rather than turn into something it hated...

A NEW DALEK ARMY

Except that it wasn't the last Dalek at all, as the Doctor and Rose were to find out. Together with Captain Jack Harkness they faced a massive Dalek fleet as it attacked Earth in the far future. The Emperor Dalek had survived after all, and using humans kidnapped from the Game Station, it built a huge new Dalek army to conquer and destroy.

The Doctor sent Rose back home so she would be safe, while he and Jack stayed to defend the Game Station and destroy the Daleks — even if that meant dying themselves, and sacrificing everyone on Earth to stop the Daleks conquering the universe. But Rose was able to open the very heart of the TARDIS and she looked into the Time Vortex and absorbed its energy. Back on the Game Station, she used that energy to destroy the entire Dalek fleet and the Emperor. It seemed that the Great Time War was indeed finally over.

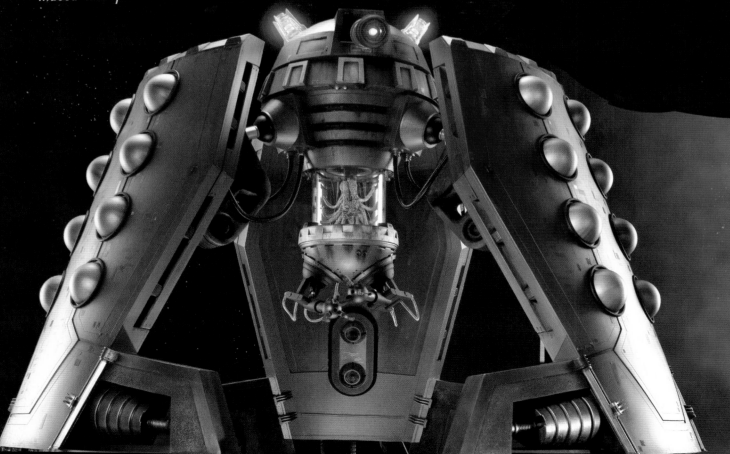

THE CULT OF SKARO

The Daleks had a secret. A secret that even the Time Lords did not know, though there were rumours and stories. As the Doctor discovered when he and Rose returned to present day Earth, these rumours were true. The so-called Cult of Skaro actually existed — a secret group of four Daleks whose job was to think the unthinkable — to dare to imagine. These Daleks even had names. They were called Sec, Thay, Jast and Caan. It was all part of becoming enough like the enemy to predict and counter their actions.

When the Daleks realised that they could not defeat the Time Lords without being totally destroyed themselves, it was the Cult of Skaro that devised a plan for survival. The four Daleks hid in the space between universes in a special Void Ship, waiting for the war to end. They took with them another secret — something they had stolen from the Time Lords themselves, something that would guarantee the survival of the Dalek race: the Genesis Ark.

Stolen from the Time Lords, the Genesis Ark was actually a prison capsule. Using Time Lord technology it was far bigger on the inside than it seemed from the outside — and was filled with thousands of Dalek prisoners of war. With Earth already invaded by millions of Cybermen, the Doctor was only just able to defeat the Daleks — and in doing so, he lost Rose...

But again, the Daleks escaped. The Cult of Skaro with their superior capabilities were able to escape using an emergency temporal shift. It used much of their power, but they managed to get to New York in the 1930s. Here they planned a very different form of invasion — turning human beings into Pig Slaves who would obey the Daleks. Then they created an army of Human Dalek Hybrids. The Dalek Commander, Sec, even bonded his form to a human's, becoming half human, half Dalek.

ONE LAST DALEK?

Once again, the Doctor was able to defeat them, this time with the help of his new friend Martha Jones. But once again, one Dalek escaped. The Doctor knows that even one Dalek can do untold damage and exterminate thousands of people. And he knows that one day he will meet that last Dalek, and then — perhaps — the Great Time War will finally be over...

SOLVE THE CLUES TO REVEAL THE NAME OF AN ALIEN RACE IN THE YELLOW BOXES.

1.
2.
3.
4.
5.
6.
7.
8.
9.
10.
11.

1. A rift in time lies under this Welsh city.
2. This race are strong, mighty, and they rock!
3. The Doctor's spaceship.
4. An alien race that hid in the centre of the Earth.
5. The Doctor's screwdriver is _ _ _ _ _.
6. The Face of _ _ _.
7. The bride the Doctor rescued.
8. The Doctor is a _ _ _ _ _ Lord.
9. The Daleks had a _ _ _ _ _ of Skaro.
10. Martha's brother.
11. The girl who helped the Doctor escape the
    Weeping Angels.

THE DOCTOR'S HOME PLANET WAS DESTROYED IN THE GREAT TIME WAR BETWEEN THE DALEKS AND THE TIME LORDS. CREATE YOUR OWN TIME WAR WITH THIS GAME OF BATTLESHIPS.

How to play:

1. Decide who is going to be the Daleks and who is going to be the Time Lords.

2. Take a piece of paper each and copy the two grids shown here on to it, one for your ships and one for your opponent's.

You will need:

Someone to play against
Pens or pencils
Paper

3. Each player places 5 ships of different sizes horizontally or vertically on the top grid.

If you are
Time Lords,
mark your
ships as:

TTTTT
TTTT
TTT
TTT
TT

If you are
Daleks, mark
your ships as:

DDDDD
DDDD
DDD
DDD
DD

Make sure your opponent can't see what you are drawing!

4. Take turns calling out a place on the grid, such as D4. The other player says "hit" if you have chosen a place with one of their ships on, or "miss" if you have not.

5. Mark your hits and misses of your opponent's ships on the second grid, with an H (hit) or an M (miss).

6. Mark your opponent's hits and misses of your ships on the top grid, with an X.

7. If your opponent manages to hit all the squares for one of your ships, then it is destroyed.

8. The first person to destroy all their opponent's ships is the winner.

BRUSH UP ON YOUR KNOWLEDGE OF THE DOCTOR'S ADVENTURES WITH THESE FUN FACTS.

ENEMIES WHO CAME BACK FOR MORE

It's amazing how some monsters come back for more even after being defeated by the Doctor...

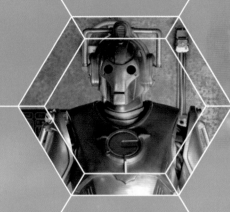

THE CYBERMEN

An enemy the Doctor has met, and defeated, on countless occasions. There are Cybermen in our universe too, so look out!

THE DALEKS

The Doctor's oldest and deadliest enemy. He first met them in his very first incarnation when he was a grumpy old man!

BLON FEL FOTCH PASAMEER-DAY SLITHEEN (ALIAS MARGARET BLAINE)

Despite the fact the Doctor defeated many of the Slitheen family, one of them came back for more — becoming Mayor of Cardiff. As if the Doctor wouldn't notice!

THE AUTONS

The Nestene Consciousness tried to invade Earth twice, and was defeated both times by the Third Doctor, long before its most recent attempt when the Doctor first met Rose.

LADY CASSANDRA O'BRIEN DOT DELTA SEVENTEEN

The Doctor and Rose met her on Platform One and then again on New Earth when Cassandra tried to steal Rose's body.

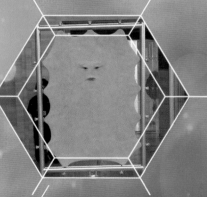

THE MASTER

Defeated by the Doctor countless times, the Master is another Time Lord and an old school mate of the Doctor's, or so it is said. You'd think he'd have learnt his lesson by now!

THE MACRA

The scourge of the galaxy, the Doctor once saved a human colony from their nasty clutches.

SOME THINGS THE SONIC SCREWDRIVER CAN DO:

It's an amazing tool with a variety of handy uses. Here's just a few of the things the Doctor can do with his sonic screwdriver:

- Fuse lift controls
- Open and lock doors
- Examine patients
- Disable security cameras
- Burn through rope

- Cut off the control signal to Nestene-controlled plastic
- Recharge mobile phone batteries and adapt phones
- Reverse teleportation
- Work the TARDIS by remote control

PLACES THE DOCTOR HAS VISITED MORE THAN ONCE

Of course the Doctor has been to Earth more times than even he can remember. But there are some other places he's paid return visits to recently:

ALBION HOSPITAL

The hospital where the Doctor first encounters the gas mask zombies is also where the Pig Pilot from the Slitheen spaceship was taken.

SATELLITE FIVE

Renamed The Game Station, the Doctor finds himself back there 100 years later.

NEW NEW YORK

Another place where things have changed in the time the Doctor's been away.

HISTORICAL FAMOUS FRIENDS AND FOES

Over the years, the Doctor has met many well-known people from history. Most recently he's run into:

- Charles Dickens — he helped the Doctor and Rose defeat the Gelth.

- Queen Victoria — the Doctor and Rose saved her from a werewolf, but she was not amused.

- Madame de Pompadour — nicknamed Reinette, she became the mistress of King Louis XV of France. The Doctor saved her from clockwork robots that were after her brain!

- William Shakespeare — helped the Doctor and Martha banish the nasty Carrionites.

- Queen Elizabeth I — has met the Doctor before, and now she wants him executed. Which was a surprise to the Doctor!

Combined brains of Mr Diagoras and Sec.

Single Dalek eye.

Human emotions.

Human body.

Ability to feel physical pain.

Webbed hands.

The Daleks created Pig Slaves out of humans they considered too stupid to be bonded with Daleks.

They conducted their genetic experiments in a secret laboratory in the Empire State Building.

MARTHA'S SHOPPING LIST

MARTHA LEFT A SHOPPING LIST BEHIND IN THE TARDIS, BUT SHE ISN'T REALLY POPPING OUT FOR GROCERIES, IT CONCEALS A CLEVER CODE!

The numbers at the beginning of each item tell you which letter in the item to look at, for example, in:

1 drink

the letter you should write down is 'd'. Look at the shopping list and work out which alien race is hidden in the words.

6 lettuces
1 yellow duster
10 packets of bacon
5 apples
15 bottles of shower gel
8 pints of milk
4 boxes of eggs
3 bananas

_ _ _ _ _ _ _

WHEN THE DOCTOR BECAME A HUMAN TO HIDE FROM THE FAMILY OF BLOOD, HE KEPT A JOURNAL OF HIS DREAMS. THESE DREAMS WERE ACTUALLY THE ADVENTURES HE HAD HAD IN REAL LIFE, AS A TIME LORD. THE JOURNAL CONTAINED DETAILS OF THE TARDIS, ROSE, AND ALL THE ALIENS AND MONSTERS THE DOCTOR HAD FOUGHT AGAINST. MAKE YOUR OWN JOURNAL OF IMPOSSIBLE THINGS FOR RECORDING YOUR DREAMS, TRAVELS AND ADVENTURES IN, BY FOLLOWING THESE SIMPLE INSTRUCTIONS:

You will need:

2 A4 sheets of thick cardboard
Sheets of A4 paper
Paints and a paintbrush
PVA glue
Sticky tape
Safe scissors
Ribbon or string
Hole punch

1 The two pieces of cardboard will be the cover of your journal. Paint or decorate both sides of them. You could cover the outsides with brown paper to make it look like an old notebook, or decorate them with your favourite stickers or pictures from magazines.

2 Cut 2 strips of paper down the length of an A4 sheet, about 3 inches wide. Paint or decorate these to match the cover of your journal. These will hold the cover together.

3 When everything is dry, place both sheets of card side by side on a flat surface, leaving a gap of about half an inch between them. Paint PVA glue down the inside length of each piece of card, then stick one of the strips of paper in place to hold the cards together and make a spine for your journal.

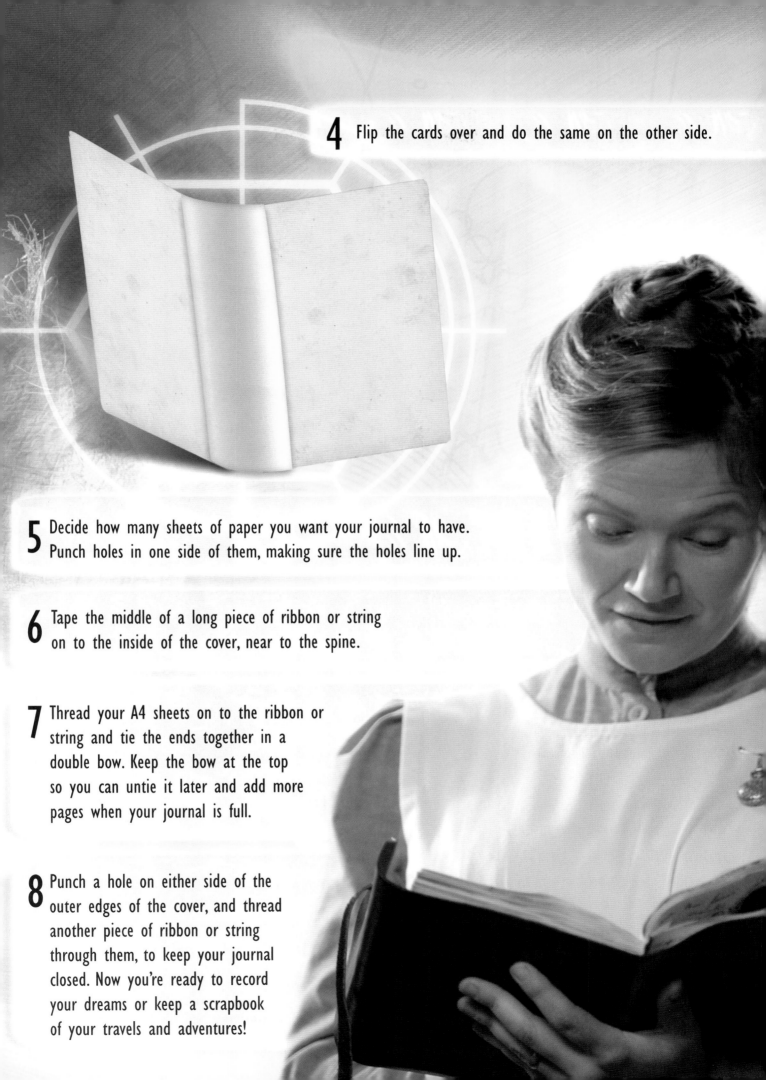

4 Flip the cards over and do the same on the other side.

5 Decide how many sheets of paper you want your journal to have. Punch holes in one side of them, making sure the holes line up.

6 Tape the middle of a long piece of ribbon or string on to the inside of the cover, near to the spine.

7 Thread your A4 sheets on to the ribbon or string and tie the ends together in a double bow. Keep the bow at the top so you can untie it later and add more pages when your journal is full.

8 Punch a hole on either side of the outer edges of the cover, and thread another piece of ribbon or string through them, to keep your journal closed. Now you're ready to record your dreams or keep a scrapbook of your travels and adventures!

THE CARRIONITES HAVE STOLEN SHAKESPEARE'S MANUSCRIPT! RACE AROUND THE BOARD TO GET IT BACK, AND BE THE ONE TO BANISH THEM BACK INTO THE DEEP DARKNESS.

Photocopy or trace the playing pieces and stick them on to cardboard. Alternatively, you can use buttons or counters.

Roll a die to see who starts. The person who rolls the highest number goes first.

Players take it in turns to roll the die and move their playing pieces forward by the number of places shown on the die. If you land on a Carrionite, move back 2 spaces.

The first player to reach the end is the winner.

WHEN THE DOCTOR'S NOT BUSY TRAVELLING TO THE ENDS OF TIME OR SAVING THE PLANET, HE LOVES SOLVING LOGIC PUZZLES! SEE IF YOU CAN HELP HIM SOLVE THESE SUDOKU PUZZLES FROM AROUND THE GALAXY.

HOW TO PLAY

Each row should contain the numbers 1-4, each column should contain the numbers 1-4, and each mini grid should contain the numbers 1-4. Fill in the missing numbers to complete the puzzles.

BILLIONS OF YEARS AGO, IN THE DARK TIMES, THE RACNOSS WOULD DEVOUR PLANETS WHOLE. THE FLEDGLING EMPIRES WENT TO WAR AGAINST THEM, AND MANAGED TO DESTROY THEM. OR SO THEY THOUGHT. TWO SHIPS SURVIVED. ONE WAS BURIED AT THE CENTRE OF THE EARTH. THE OTHER, CONTAINING THE EMPRESS OF THE RACNOSS, FLED TO THE EDGE OF THE UNIVERSE AND DRIFTED IN SILENCE, WAITING FOR THE RIGHT TIME TO WAKE HER CHILDREN FROM HIBERNATION...

Numerous eyes.

Sharp fangs.

Massive abdomen.

Donna's husband-to-be, Lance Bennett, was the Empress' consort and fed Donna the Huon Particles that would allow her to b used as the key to open the Secret Heart — the sh at the centre of the Earth

10ft long legs.

2 arms, 6 legs.

PAGE 9 - DALEK WORDSEARCH

(word search grid)

W	R	Y	I	O	P	L	G	D	A	C	N	M	V	E
X	I	C	U	L	T	O	H	J	K	R	T	S	T	B
M	F	A	Z	G	Y	U	T	F	R	D	E	A	E	N
R	S	A	O	O	D	A	L	U	J	H	N	C	R	V
G	E	N	E	S	I	S	A	R	K	I	P	O	P	I
K	C	D	M	F	N	O	P	E	M	G	E	D	S	L
J	A	S	P	T	H	A	L	R	S	C	A	J	A	N
S	K	Z	E	K	L	A	E	B	K	J	S	A	T	S
E	C	F	R	Y	D	T	B	V	A	J	L	S	Y	O
T	G	R	O	A	X	Y	S	K	R	I	E	T	S	M
A	H	K	R	E	N	E	W	Y	O	R	K	E	M	E
S	A	A	D	U	Y	T	R	E	S	D	G	H	N	B
K	L	D	Y	P	I	G	S	L	A	V	E	S	M	E

PAGE 32 - CHRISTMAS QUIZ

1. False, 2. B, 3. C, 4. A, 5. C, 6. B, 7. True,
8. True, 9. C, 10. A, 11. False, 12. C,
13. A. The Sycorax, B. A Robot Santa, C. The Empress of the Racnoss

PAGE 23 - WATCH HUNT

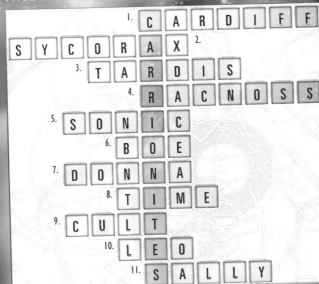

PAGE 47 - ALIEN GRID

1. CARDIFF
2. SYCORAX
3. TARDIS
4. RACNOSS
5. SONIC
6. BOE
7. DONNA
8. TIME
9. CULT
10. LEO
11. SALLY

PAGE 34 - CAPTAIN JACK'S CONUNDRUM

The code translates to say:

He used a Vortex Manipulator to travel back in time and wait to see the Doctor again.

PAGE 53 - MARTHA'S SHOPPING LIST

CYBERMEN

PAGE 58 - SO-DOC-WHO

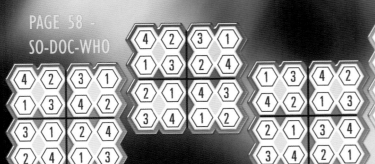